大師

The
Master

大師

CHAO-HSIU CHEN

The

aster

THE WAY TO FULFILMENT

BOOK PUBLISHING

A CONNECTIONS EDITION

This edition published in Great Britain in 2002 by
Connections Book Publishing Limited
St Chad's House, 148 King's Cross Road, London WC1X 9DH

This edition published in the U.S.A. in 2002 by
Connections Book Publishing Limited.
Distributed in the U.S.A. by Red Wheel/Weiser,
368 Congress Street, Boston, MA 02210

British Library Cataloguing-in-Publication data available on request.

ISBN 1-85906-088-9

1 3 5 7 9 10 8 6 4 2

English translation by Doris and Robert Allen
Editorial: Mary Lambert, Liz Wheeler
Design: Hayley Cove, Malcolm Smythe
Production: Karyn Claridge, Charles James
Phototypset in Bell MT using Quark XPress on Apple Macintosh
Origination by Bright Arts, Singapore
Printed in Italy by Amadeus Industria Poligrafica Europea, Rome

CONTENTS

CONTENTS

Wherever he went, his stick left a trace.

MOUNTAINS, MOUNTAINS EVERYWHERE ... and in the midst, a lake.

A lonely figure stands on the summit, casting a glance at the harsh, snow-covered rocks and the freezing water which begs the wind for a last wave.

A rushing sound can be heard on all sides. In the sky clouds flow past as though borne on the ever-changing stream of life. The paths that have led him here were stony and thick with dust. Wherever he went, his stick left a trace. Now his eyes know no more longing, his heart weeps no more tears. Though surrounded by the cold he does not feel it because he is warmed by his memories. He grasps the sandalwood stick which his Master left him and which he took with him on the path of wisdom. He recalls the love of the girl who once helped him to find the right way, and he hears the words, which once called out to him: *'My child ...'*

The life of the village follows its own rules.

SPRING HAD JUST returned. Even so, the winter had not yet lost its power and still sent strong, cold winds from the mountains. The village shopkeeper had hung curtains across the entrance, so dark and heavy that no one could see in. It was warm inside. At the inn they made do without such protection, but instead the entrance had been reinforced with heavy beams. This, however, was not enough to prevent the wind from blowing dust from the street over and under the door. The teams of mules that passed by outside also kicked up the dry ground with their hooves and created further clouds of dust in the air.

When the wind dropped and the sun warmed the air, the children came out of the huts and houses to play in the village square. Stray dogs roamed around attempting to hunt the chickens. Women with colourful scarves tied around their hair hurried to the market to buy rice, vegetables and dried fish. The life of the village followed its own rules and the rhythm of the seasons. People were used to a simple life where there was little news. Nothing much happened except the occasional celebration of a wedding or a death. Only once was there great excitement and this was when the first ever gaslights were lit on the market square.

I try to create something wonderful out of something worthless.

H E LEFT HIS father's house and went to the village square to play with his friends. When he arrived at the fountain he noticed a strange knocking noise. At first he had no idea where it came from. Then he realized that it was being made by the stick carried by an old man as he descended the temple steps. The wind blew his long hair and ruffled his shining silver beard. The boy was impressed, he had never seen anyone like this before. The knocking came closer and, through a gap in the clouds, sunshine fell on the face of the old man who seemed to radiate experience of life.

The boy stared at the stranger. It was a rare event indeed for an outsider to come to the village. His shoes and clothes were tattered and worn because, the boy supposed, he must have crossed many mountains and rivers in order to get here. At this moment the other children also saw the new arrival.

'Who are you and where do you come from?' they wanted to know.

'I don't have a name any more,' answered the man, 'and I don't know which way led me here. Last night I slept where the sun went down and this morning I awoke where it rose.'

The children laughed at his strange words and wanted to hear more.

'Who have you met on your way?' asked a girl.

'I met two kinds of people. One created something wonderful out of something worthless and the other made something worthless out of something wonderful.'

'And which type are you?' queried the girl.

'I try to create something wonderful out of something worthless. Then something worthless out of something wonderful ánd, then from the worthless, something wonderful again.'

'I don't understand that,' said a boy. 'Does it mean that you can make something which has broken become complete again?'

'I'm sure that you could do it too,' replied the old man.

Another boy said, 'I can't do it because my father always calls me "Strawhead", even when I do something right.'

The children began to debate. The more they talked, the louder and more excited they became, and they crowded around the old man. They felt that he was different from the other village men. Suddenly a rough voice called out:

'Hey, you! Strawhead! Are you still here? Go home now!'

The boy who'd been told off inclined his head and turned to go. Some of the others followed him because it was also time for them to return home.

'My mother says that there's no place like home,' a girl said collecting her toys, 'and my grandparents say it as well.'

The old man looked at the girl thoughtfully.

'If your parents regard the house in which they live as their most important possession, then they live in shackles. That's why it is better to regard the home in which you live as a hostel in which you spend one day after another.'

'So where is your hostel?' asked the boy who had first discovered the old man.

'It is as far away as the end of the sky, and as near as the beginning of the earth. It is where the heart finds its peace.'

Everyone is born with different gifts.

THE SUN ROSE over the village and sent her first rays to give energy for a new day. The people started preparing the first meal of their day.

After the boy had finished eating he ran to the village as fast as he could to look for the strange man. He only found a mule driver who led three of his animals to the meadow. He had put his child on to the first one and he directed the animal with a little stick.

At that moment the old man appeared. The mule driver went up to him and said, 'Why have my parents left me with such a hard destiny? Since childhood I've had to look after the animals and make sure that they were strong enough to carry heavy loads over the mountains. I have inherited nothing but labour and poverty. Why did I choose such parents?'

Turning to the boy he then added, 'You can be happy. Your family has been the head of the village for generations. They are wealthy and respected by everyone. You can't imagine what it's like to try to make do with one meal a day.'

The old man pulled some dried apricots out of his bag and shared them between the mule driver, his child and the animals. Then he said:

'Everyone is born with different gifts, for which the parents are not responsible. Those who have chosen a hard destiny for themselves have to work harder the greater their ambition. He who has chosen an easy destiny has to develop further because there is nothing he has to strive for apart from gratitude towards his parents. He who can achieve this will be happy.'

He stopped for a moment and then carried on in a serious voice, 'Unfortunately this will usually be realized only when our parents have left us.'

In the meantime the boys' friends had arrived and were following the conversation. The mule driver looked at the children angrily and asked:

'Why are some of them obedient but others can't be tamed?

Then the old man raised his voice and said, 'Children are your guilt towards life. They come to rescue you and their task is not to fulfil your wishes because it is their wish that you help them to become what they really are.' And in a forceful voice he finished his words, saying, 'Unfortunately this is usually only understood when you have already entered the wrong path.'

Look at the sky!

EVERYTHING THE BOY had heard so far sounded familiar, although such words had never reached his ears before. An inner voice told him that it was important to learn more. He looked for the old man everywhere and discovered him finally at the river. He lay on the ground and stared at the sky.

'What are you doing there?' asked the boy anxiously.

'I am studying nature,' replied the old man, 'I feel the sun, hear the water, and see the clouds.'

'And why do you do that?'

'Because it is the best way to remove the inner dust,' came the answer.

'I'm afraid I don't understand you.'

The old man got up, took a deep breath, and said:

'Each person carries a great wisdom in himself, but nobody finds this ancient treasure because it is buried under mountains of grief. Once you learn to remove the rubble of sorrow and pain, you can see the treasure gleam in the light of the eternal sun. The frozen tears of life will thaw and wisdom and blissfulness will awake.'

After he had stopped for a moment, he said to the boy:

'Look at the sky, can you see the sun?'

'No,' answered the boy, 'I see only clouds.'

'So where is the sun?' asked the old man forcefully.

'It's hidden behind the clouds.'

Then the old man said, 'Even if the clouds cover the sun, they are not able to stop the light and warmth. The clouds are the rubble and the sun is the wisdom.'

'I have understood what you mean but it is still not clear to me how you can manage to remove the rubble from the Treasure of Life,' objected the boy.

'If you really want I will let you in on the secret,' promised the man. 'But you will have to give up everything for that. You will have to leave your home, your parents, your brothers and sisters …'

'… and also my friends?' asked the boy anxiously, but at the same time full of hope that one day he would return home with mighty riches.

'My child,' replied the old man smiling, 'this is only the first step ...'

*Everything tastes good if it is prepared with respect and
eaten with gratitude.*

SOON IT WAS noon. For days the boy and the Master went on their way. They walked over snow fields, looked for places to sleep in the woods, and climbed through gorges until they left the cold breath of the mountains behind. Now a valley opened in front of them whose terraced fields intertwined with numerous streams and alternated with juicy meadows in between the dispersed huts and farms. In the distance they saw how the farmers worked in their fields whilst their wives fed the fires in front of their houses with wood in order to prepare meals.

The boy followed the Master, who made his way towards one of the huts. They brought out their bowls and asked for a donation.

'I am ashamed, Master,' wailed the boy, 'at always having to beg.'

The Master laughed: 'You are not begging; just the opposite. In allowing someone to give you something, you help him perform a good deed.'

'And what of those who don't even have enough to feed themselves?' retorted the boy. 'Should they also give something to us?'

'We have to give those people something,' answered the Master.

'But how can we give if we have nothing ourselves?'

'By going begging for them.'

The two wanderers sat down at a meadow and started to eat. The Master noticed that the boy looked at his meal without enthusiasm.

'Don't you like it?' he asked.

'It tastes awful!' answered the boy peevishly, as he thought of the richly laid table in his parents' house.

'Everything tastes good if it is prepared with respect and eaten with gratitude.' With these words the Master brought his pupil back to reality and he noticed that the boy looked down in embarrassment. He put his arm around him and continued:

'Someone has given us some rice. Let us try to honour this gift. Put one grain of rice in your mouth and close your eyes. Can you feel the field where it grew? Can you taste the sky guarding the earth? And can you taste the universe that grows in you?

After a while the pupil opened his eyes and said:

'That was the best rice that I have ever eaten.'

Nobody can live without care.

THICK, GREY RAIN clouds had appeared in the sky. Although it was early in the day it seemed as if it was nearly night time. Nature had collected all its power and threatened to unleash it at any moment.

The path, on which the thick snow had now melted, had become virtually impassable. The Master and his pupil plodded through the deep mud. They came across a flock of sheep. The animals stood closely together. The shepherd had picked up a lamb that had got separated from its flock and brought it back on his horse. When he saw the two figures approaching he was happy about the unexpected visitors, especially as it had now become lighter and the expected thunder and lightning appeared to have moved away. He rode towards them and offered them fresh cheese from his saddlebag as a welcome. The Master folded his hands together in front of his chest and thanked the shepherd with a slight bow. The boy did likewise and asked the man:

'Do you live here all alone?'

'No,' he answered. 'As you see, I live with my sheep.'

'But haven't you any parents or relatives?'

'No.'

'You must be terribly lonely,' said the boy. He noticed suddenly how much he missed his parents and his brothers and sisters.

'Not at all,' laughed the shepherd. 'I am not lonely, I am free.'

'None of us is free,' the Master retorted. 'We are like your sheep. Nobody can live without care. We all depend on each other and that's why we all have to carry some responsibility.'

'But that means that there is no freedom,' the boy retorted.

'Freedom is like the air. You can neither see nor hear it, and when it touches you, you do not know how to appreciate it. But if you lose it, then you begin to miss it. Do you think that a free man can do whatever he likes? No, because he has to carry his own share of responsibility, just like the shepherd who looks after his animals.'

'But it is obvious that I really care for them,' said the shepherd.

'And it is just because of that that you remain free,' replied the Master, looking thoughtfully at his young pupil.

The thunderstorm approached once more and the pair went on their way.

Everything happens because it has to happen.

O NE DAY, THE Master and his pupil came to a village in which almost every house bordered a magnificent orchard. From everywhere came the wonderful scent of peach, almond and apricot blossoms. The excitement of spring was in the air.

In one of the gardens they came across a young girl picking flowers. Every time she bent down, her long, black plait brushed the earth. Her silhouette put one in mind of a precious vase made of the finest porcelain. As the boy watched her he felt, for the very first time, a powerful longing. It was a feeling he had never experienced before, both happy and painful at the same time. At this moment the girl left the garden and, as she passed the two wanderers, shyly lowered her gaze.

'Master,' asked the boy, 'shall we follow her home to ask for a meal?'

The Master didn't answer and the girl disappeared from view. The pair continued down the road until they came to the first house. They knocked to attract attention but no one came. Just then a blind old man appeared from the rather dilapidated house next door.

'Who are you?' he called out. 'Come in and have a meal with us!'

The Master took the boy's hand and led him inside. Despite the poor appearance of the exterior, inside the house was warm, comfortable, clean and light. They saw the girl they had just met in the garden kneeling to put wood on the fire.

'My granddaughter told me that you were here,' the blind man said. 'Find yourselves somewhere to sit and the meal will be ready soon.'

As the young pupil took his place at the table, he stole a glance at the girl's face. He was so enchanted by her beauty that he forgot to sit down and instead stood rooted to the spot.

'Sit down,' he heard the Master say.

'I live here alone except for my granddaughter,' said the blind man. 'At first, I looked after her because her parents were killed in an avalanche many years ago. Now that I have lost my sight it is she who looks after me, and she spoils me so much that I am happy to be blind.'

'It is a cause for rejoicing when we no longer have to look on the woes of the world,' replied the Master.

'You must know a lot about life,' said the girl. 'Can you tell me whether I will one day see my parents again?'

For a while there was silence in the room. Then the Master said:

'There is no death in life. Everything is change. The leaves fall from the tree and turn into earth, which helps a new tree to grow.'

'But people are not trees,' the boy retorted.

'All is one,' replied the Master. 'Everything is governed by the same law. Everything passes according to that law and everything returns according to that law. The river of change runs in us all at this moment, and the next, and the one after that. We are all just drops in its flow.'

'And what about love?' the boy wanted to know. 'Is it also subject to the law?'

'Love is always there even when it appears to be absent,' answered the Master.

The grandfather, who was sitting between the Master and the boy, said:

'Whatever will happen, we can't avoid it. And whatever won't happen, we can't force it. Everything happens because it has to happen.'

Later, when they resumed their journey, the boy glanced back longingly at the girl's house.

Turn the power of destruction into the power of the good.

THE MASTER AND his pupil had travelled far when, one day, they reached a desert which seemed to stretch forever at the foot of a range of mountains. The sand was mixed with stones but, when the first rays of the sun managed to break through the clouds, the hills that appeared dark grey became a golden, shining sea with softly dancing waves.

The wanderers had to cross this place in order to reach another high mountain range on the other side. Day after day they travelled. To save their strength they hardly talked to each other. They communicated with glances and when they took a break they stayed no longer than strictly necessary because they did not know how long it would take them to reach their destination. Some days sand seemed to change into snow, but it was really only the heat that made it appear to be gleaming white. In this heat the boy nearly despaired. Matters were made worse by the intense cold that descended on the plain at night. The Master taught him to cultivate resistance to hunger and thirst, heat and cold and, in this way, to cultivate the strength required to reach his goal.

Suddenly the sun disappeared and one could hardly feel the heat any more. When the boy looked round he saw that a huge black dust cloud was approaching rapidly. It was still some distance away but, even so, there was hardly enough time to reach the cover of the mountains before the storm struck. As the storm rushed towards them, the Master stopped and turned. He spread out his arms and called in a voice that made the boy shudder:

'Storm! Brother Storm! Let all your anger and hate become visible and turn the power of destruction into the power of something good. Hasten to where you are needed. Find your freedom by making yourself useful. And now show yourself again in your whole splendour!'

The Master had hardly spoken these words when the storm raged above him and the boy. It whipped up the sand with such force that it seemed as if eternal night was covering the world. The boy shouted desperately for help. From what seemed to come from a great distance he heard these words:

'Take the end of the stick and hold on to it! If we both hold the stick we can reach the next rock and find shelter from the storm.'

The boy grabbed hold of the stick and they ran as fast as they could towards the safety of the mountains. But the boy's fear grew. The rocks seemed further away than they had supposed. The sand got into his eyes and ears, and filled his nose. It covered him completely and left no possibility of escape. He held on to the Master's stick as best he could because he knew that if he let go they would both be lost. Then, through the raging storm, he heard a voice that called to him, 'Don't let go! You've nearly reached it! Hold on a just a bit longer!'

Suddenly the boy felt stones under his feet and noticed how the storm gradually lessened. There was now less sand in the air. Slowly he opened his eyes but, to his alarm, he saw nothing but dreary darkness. They found themselves in a cave at the foot of the mountains. There was just a narrow passage that led into the interior. The Master had obviously known of this cave, because he said:

'Here I often have a whole conversation with Brother Storm. He clearly knows that he should keep his temper in check but he doesn't always succeed. He is full of energy but fails to recognize when he should use it. At one time he and his sister, the Water, liked to play at hollowing out the rocks. That's why the place is so full of chasms and caves, each one deeper than the last. Some are so spacious that they take days to explore completely.'

For one moment, the boy hoped that the Master had brought him here because he knew of a treasure in one of the caves which he should help him to recover.

Then the Master said, 'Here we will find nothing but the wounds of the earth.'

When the boy had got used to the dark, he saw that the walls of the cave were divided by empty recesses of different sizes.

'A long time ago there were statues all around,' said the Master, 'made by pilgrims who came here in search of the Treasure of Life. On their journey they rested to renew their mental and physical strength. As a show of gratitude, and an offering to those who would follow, they left artwork beaten into the rock. These were so artistically done that soon their fame spread far and wide.'

'So why are the recesses all empty now?' the boy asked.

'Because there are people who take things that do not belong to them and they sell them. Then they use the money to buy things they believe they need, and the coins are suddenly in the possession of others without ever changing anything.'

The Master stopped for a moment, then continued:

'One day all the statues will be turned to sand once more and Brother Storm will carry them to wonderful regions and inhospitable shores. He leaves you and me here, and we continue our journey, but one day we too will turn to grains of sand and, having been mixed with others, we will be carried off by Brother Storm until, at last, we are reborn.'

In the meantime the storm had abated and the Master and his pupil prepared to leave the cave. When they reached the exit the boy said, 'Where are we going now?'

The Master answered very quietly, 'We are going to where the treasure can be found.'

Have confidence in yourself.

THE STORM HAD blown so much sand into the cave that the Master and his pupil found it difficult to leave their refuge. Outside, the world had changed. In places where sand and rocks had been lying in heaps, everything was blown flat. In other places, where the going had been easy, there were now sand dunes. It was hard to find one's way because all the former landmarks had now been changed. At last the Master found a path beside the mountains that would lead eventually to the next human settlement.

As they were passing one of the numerous caves, they saw a horse whose reins were tethered to a large rock. The owner was nowhere to be seen.

'The animal obviously belonged to someone who came here in search of the statues,' said the Master,' someone who would certainly not appreciate any eyewitnesses.'

'In that case we are in danger here,' answered the boy. 'Let's move on as fast as we can!'

'No,' said the Master, and made himself comfortable next to the horse. 'As long as you have no fear, danger will avoid you. So let's wait until the owner turns up.'

It didn't take long for a boy dressed in rags, and not much

older than the pupil, to appear. Startled, he asked, 'What are you doing here?'

'We've been waiting for you,' said the pupil.

'Why?'

'Because we wanted to know what you were looking for inside the mountains.'

The boy took a bulging sack from his shoulder and, hanging his head in embarrassment, said, 'Why do you want to know?'

'We believe that you want to take away ancient treasures from the mountain,' said the Master in a strict voice.

'It's nothing to do with you and, anyway, the statues don't belong to anybody,' retorted the boy.

The Master got up and said, 'What belongs to nobody, you can't carry away. Do you think you could ever really own a piece of land?'

'Of course, if I fenced it in.'

'But can you also carry it away?'

'No, but I could stay within my fence.'

'Very good,' said the Master. 'If you think that the statue belongs to you, then take it back to where you found it and stay with it forever.'

The strange boy remained silent and perplexed. Then he bowed to the Master, 'I have understood.' He turned and made his way back to the cave. He returned with his sack empty and the Master put everything he had left to eat into it.

'What shall I do when the sack is empty once more?' asked the boy.

'Have confidence in yourself and the sack will never be empty, especially if you don't steal.' Then he said goodbye to the boy and, accompanied by his pupil, continued on his way.

Don't lose your faith.

THEY CONTINUED TO travel day after day until they saw signs of a settlement. The landscape grew gentler and the scenery more beautiful.

The pupil was thankful that his hunger and thirst would soon be satisfied. He felt absolutely worn out. His clothes and shoes were torn and dirty and he hadn't been able to wash himself for a long time. He regretted having left his safe home and was longing for a return to his family.

When the Master noticed how tired and sulky his pupil was, he said, 'Don't lose your faith. You have more energy than me and I'm sure that we will soon be able to get something to eat.'

At that moment a woman approached them and invited the travellers to rest and refresh themselves in her husband's house. She reminded the boy of his mother and his longing became even stronger. The joy of finding himself once more in a sheltered place, however, lessened his ill humour.

After they had washed and eaten, the woman wanted to show them to the sleeping quarters. But the Master said, 'I thank you but do not want to be a burden on you. Tonight we will sleep on the earth in the arms of our

Mother, because tomorrow we must be without her for some time.'

They left the house at dusk. The colours of the sky were clear and the landscape lay silently before them. When the moon lit up the distant land, the boy noticed his own shadow and was surprised how tall he had become. Then he glanced at the shadow of his Master, and at that moment he had a premonition that they would not reach the end of the path that stretched before them for a very long time.

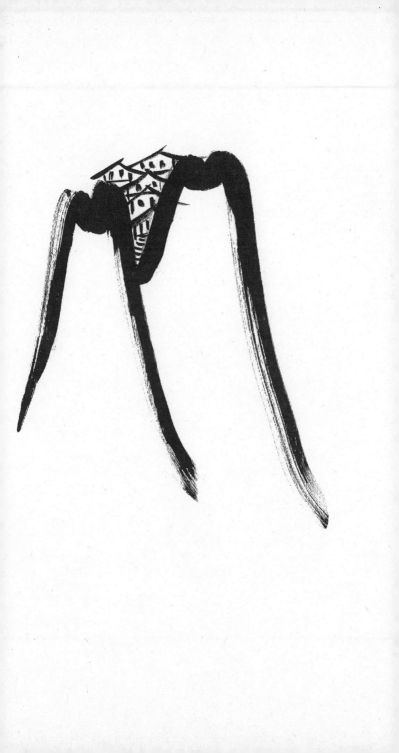

Each house was crowned with a golden roof.

WHEN THE BOY woke up he saw his Master deep in meditation. His face pointed towards where the sun would soon rise and his hands lay like shells on his knees. The boy jumped up and ran to the brook to wash himself. Then he laid out his gown. The sun dappled the landscape, the air was cool and fresh, and only a few little clouds scudded by in the sky.

The Master didn't say a word when the pupil approached him. He only raised his stick and pointed in the direction that they had to travel.

The path was difficult and they made slow progress. Time and again huge pillars of rock hindered their way, and they had to leave the main path so that they could find a place where it was possible to climb up to the temple. They were faced with almost impassable woods and gorges.

Eventually they came to a lake that lay below a mighty mountain. The boy knelt and scooped up water in his hands. Then he noticed something golden gleaming as it was blown towards them by the wind. He looked up and stared above. On a rock spur the majestic site of an ancient temple could be seen. It was so magnificent that he was completely overawed.

As they climbed towards it he could not be sure, but it looked as though the temple consisted of a few large and several small buildings. Each house had a golden roof with artistically curved edges that were upturned, as though they intended to take leave of the earth altogether. A wall decorated with pagodas surrounded the whole site. It looked as though it was intended to protect the inhabitants from wild animals.

The two wanderers entered the temple. The boy's heart was filled with respect and curiosity. He followed the Master across a set of broad stairs and into a prayer room. As the room was empty, they went to an annexe in which there was a workshop where some monks were inspecting old manuscripts for signs of damage.

The eldest monk rose and approached the newcomers and, bowing, greeted them:

'Welcome! We expected you to arrive earlier but we heard that you were delayed by a sandstorm. It is good that you have survived unhurt. I have everything prepared for you already.'

The Master bowed as well and thanked him for his kindness. Then he encouraged the pupil to kneel and pay his respects to the old monk. Afterwards he was instructed in the rules of the cloisters. The old monk said, 'In this holy place, we monks must strengthen not only our spirit but also our bodies, as we believe that neither can be neglected because we need both to live. In addition, we practise the art of inner immersion, and also we pay heed to the voice of nature. Humans often live too hastily so that they overlook things that are really important. In the cloisters you learn how to appreciate a slower pace, because in that way you can learn to see, hear, taste, smell and feel.'

A young monk led them through the garden to their chamber. A great tiredness overcame the pupil and his Master advised him to lie down and sleep. Eventually a bell rang that indicated the end of the night's sleep. The Master pulled aside a curtain that separated his cubicle from that of the boy. He saw that his pupil was still fast asleep. In spite of that, he woke him up to go to morning prayers. They entered a prayer hall and saw that it was full almost to the last seat. Even so, monks dressed in wide, flowing gowns were entering from all sides. As light gradually filtered into the room, it took on the colour of the monks' robes and soon the place was bathed in a colourful atmosphere of contemplation.

In the beginning everyone prayed quietly on his own until the novices started to sing to the accompaniment of some instruments in order to pray together for the enlightening of the hearts.

Later they all went to their separate tasks. Some had to work in the kitchen, others in the garden and yet others had to climb down to a well part of the way down the mountain and carry back water for the temple. Several monks practised the art of mindfulness whilst cleaning. Others devoted themselves to the study of old manuscripts in order to broaden their knowledge. As the boy hadn't been given a particular task, he followed the Master back to their chamber. The Master asked him to make tea and bring it to the desk. The boy did as he was asked and then lay down on his bed and started to think about his new home. Suddenly the hissing of the boiling kettle dragged him from his thoughts. The Master said to him, 'Most people are like the water in a kettle. They try to reach boiling point but, when this has happened, they don't think about removing the kettle from the fire. That is why the water boils over and extinguishes exactly that which brought it to the boil.'

'And what happens if the water is kept continuously on the boil without extinguishing the fire?' asked the boy.

'Then it turns to steam, which disperses in the air, but can you get hold of air?'

'Of course not,' answered the boy.

The Master continued, 'But the steam can return to you.'

'How so?'

'It has the ability to change into rain. But can we be sure that the water of the rain is the same as that which came from the tea kettle?'

'No,' replied the boy, 'that is impossible.'

'The path of water,' continued the Master, 'is also the path of life. Parents think that their children belong to them. Children think that as soon as they grow up their bodies are their own. Everybody looks after his goods and chattels. But no matter how carefully you guard your possessions, everything you own will eventually leave you and no one can prevent it. Children leave their parents, our souls leave our bodies, and all that we accomplish will eventually be lost and there is nothing we can do about it. That is why it's good to live like the water.'

So then it was the Master who boiled the water for the tea.

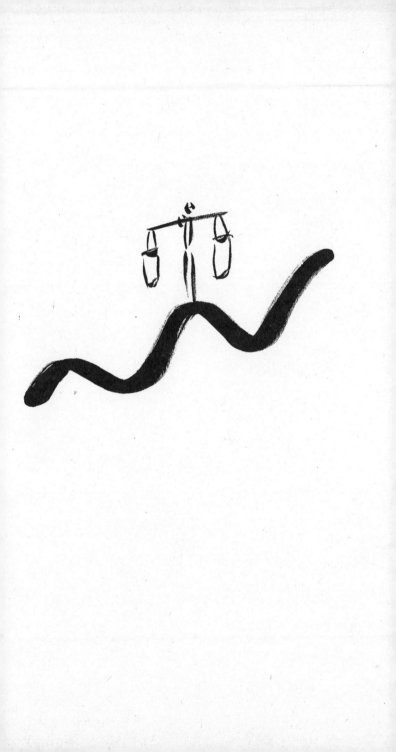

In the temple the boy learned the secret of timelessness.

D AYS, WEEKS, MONTHS and years went by. In the temple the boy learned the secret of timelessness. Nothing changed, everything moved at a steady pace. The mental and physical exercises were repeated almost hourly and it seemed to him that his world followed a law which had existed unchanging since ancient times. He had to pray, to study, to clean, to cook and to write. He also had to learn how to defend himself and to keep his feelings under control. He had to carry out both the simplest and the most difficult of tasks at the same time.

Gradually, he became familiar with the rules of the temple. One of these was that the novices had to fetch all the water that was needed in the temple by bucket from the well. For this purpose, each novice had a bamboo yoke to place over his shoulder and, on each end, a wooden vessel hung.

One morning, as he returned through the thick snow to the temple wearing only canvas shoes on his feet, the Master said to him, 'When you have learned to forget yourself, you will not feel the pain any more. And when you have learned to renounce distraction, you will already have forgotten yourself.'

'But what is wrong with distracting yourself?' the boy asked.

The Master laughed, full of understanding, 'In order to find the Treasure of Life, it is necessary to keep away from the Tree of Sorrow. This tree grows in the same way as lust. If you only trim off the branches, others will soon grow. That is why it is necessary to pull the tree up by its roots and destroy it. In this way you can master your passions, the good as well as the bad.'

When they arrived in the temple, the boy emptied his load in the water cistern and then ran as fast as he could back to the well. When the Master saw that he was overzealous, he asked him, 'Do you think that the sun goes down earlier just because you want to get to bed sooner?'

No one is a thief by nature.

IN TIME, THE pupil found pleasure in his life at the temple. Even the prayer hour in the evening now brought him fulfilment, and he was always eager to experience the way in which the chants of the monks united with the sounds of nature.

One evening the Master asked him, 'How is your art of water-carrying coming on? '

'I'm becoming much faster.'

'Are you faster than the water?'

'It's my steps that are faster.'

The Master answered, ' If you want to overcome yourself, you have to become one with the water. You must be neither faster nor slower. In order to reach the goal, all the mental and physical exercises you have learned here are necessary. The mental ones help you to forget the difference between that which is internal, external and physical. When you have gained expertise in both types of exercise, you will also have overcome sorrow, because sorrow is you. You and it are one and the same. Beyond sorrow you will find the wisdom that is anxious to receive you.'

In the weeks that followed the pupil had to learn more than ever before. He retreated into the library, which was situated in a pagoda and was filled to the ceiling with manuscripts from many countries. There he spent most of the day. He found old manuscripts and greedily absorbed their wisdom. He read many books that were written by the monks of the temple, and he learned and began to understand.

He just wanted to enter completely into one such old book, whose writing was carved in bamboo. Then he heard a great uproar, which appeared to come from the room above the library in which the most valuable manuscripts were kept. The boy was startled so he jumped up and ran up the stairs, where he found several monks trying to detain a thief who had been attempting to steal one of the manuscripts, and was now desperately defending himself and trying to avoid capture.

The pupil rushed to help the monks and recognized the intruder as the boy who, after the great sand storm, had wanted to steal a statue from the mountain caves. After he had been overcome they dragged him before the abbot, who told him, 'Whoever offends against the law must be punished.' The Master entered the room and immediately he also recognized the thief. He said, 'There are people who steal for the sake of stealing but there are also those who steal because they are in dire straits and find themselves in misery. If one punishes the first sort one fulfils the requirements of the law, but if one punishes the second sort one makes their situation even worse.'

As the Master was held in high regard at the temple no one dared to contradict him, but the abbot asked, 'Don't you know that the river whose course you change will one day cause great damage?' How can you want to change the law?'

'If a river bursts its banks each year, is it not better to dig a new course instead of trying vainly to keep it within its present banks with sandbags?' countered the Master.

'I think that's right,' agreed the abbot, 'but can you tell me how to create a new course for the river?'

'This young man, whom my pupil and I have met before, is no thief by nature. No one is born a thief. It is always life that causes someone to take what is not his. That is why punishment has to be used in such a way that it will give him the opportunity to make reparations for his deed and also open up new ways for the fulfilment of his being. That is why I advise that you keep the boy in the temple and teach him everything you know. In exchange he will help with all tasks that are not part of the duties of the monks. Also you should ask him why he became a thief.'

The boy stepped in front of the Master, bowed deeply, and said, 'Master, I haven't forgotten your words from before, but unfortunately I have only rarely been able to keep my sack full in an honourable way. But you are right, nobody is born a thief by nature and neither am I, but in spite of that, life has made me one. I beg you, and all the monks, to listen to my story. Many years ago my parents' house burned to the ground. Nobody survived apart from me and my two younger brothers, whom I managed to save from the flames. For my parents, help came too late. Although there were many rich people in our village, nobody saw the need to support us orphans and to lessen our pain. Nobody gave me work because they said I was too small for it. But I had to look after my two brothers and myself. So I started to steal chickens and ducks. But that wasn't enough, especially in the winter. One day two strangers came to our village, a man and a woman. They were looking for old art objects. As I knew where such things could be found, I took these two aside and offered to get them what they wanted in return for money. When they left our village they wanted to take my brothers with them, but not me because I was already too old. As I had a duty to look after my younger brothers as best I could, I let them go with the strangers.'

The boy paused and sighed. Then he continued, 'In certain circles I was known for my "work" and therefore sometimes people commissioned me to find old statues for them. I could live longer on the proceeds of such a theft than I could from stealing chickens and ducks, so my thefts became rarer but probably with much graver consequences.'

The Master's pupil listened to the boy's words with sympathy. He said, 'You crossed mountains and rivers and faced many dangers to get here and steal these ancient manuscripts. Why are they so valuable?'

'I have no idea. I have been told that these are the oldest and rarest writings anywhere in the world.'

The Master asked him, 'If this theft had been successful, would you then have stopped stealing?'

'Of course! They would have given me so much money that I would never have had to steal again.'

After a moment's silence the Master said, 'Good. Now you know where the manuscripts are kept. If you still want them, nobody will stop you from taking them.'

They all left the room apart from the pupil, who said to the boy, 'I have made huge efforts and even left my family to follow the Master in order to find the Treasure of Life. For months I have studied in this library and didn't notice that what I was looking for was nearby. I thank you for opening my eyes. Now I finally know why the Master has brought me here.'

'I don't think that this is the Treasure of Life that you're seeking,' said the boy, 'because if it was you surely couldn't steal it so easily.'

'But where is it, then? ' asked the pupil, who suddenly felt unsure again.

'Have confidence in yourself. Surely the Master knows, otherwise he wouldn't have brought you with him. And now show me how you live here.'

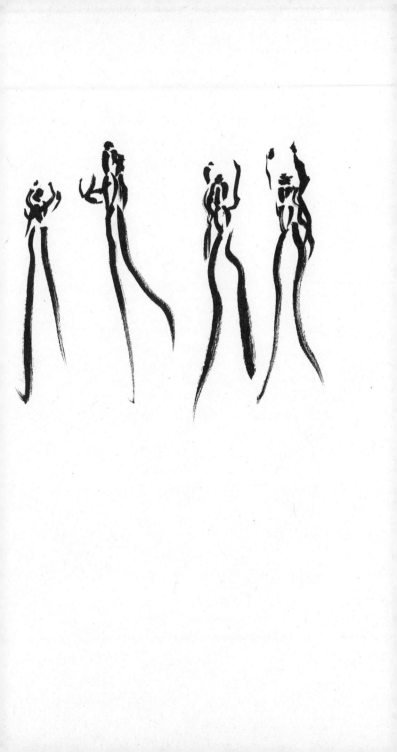

In the House of the Scented Jasmine.

TORMENTED BY DOUBTS the young thief went into a deep sleep. Next morning he was unsure whether he should be happy or disappointed. Despite that, for the first time in his life he took part in morning prayers. And for the first time he did not have to feel sorrowful about the way he supported himself. He soon adapted to the way of life in the temple and day by day he got used to leading a life free of sorrow. One day, when the stores of the temple were nearly exhausted, the abbot sent both boys to go shopping in a nearby town. The administrator of the temple gave them the necessary money and ordered them to be back in three days' time. The pupil was happy about this because he had not been outside the temple precincts since his arrival there. Now he was not only going to see something new, but he also had a friend of the same age.

On the way the young thief said, 'Now I'll broaden your horizons and show you the life I lived before. The existence of a thief may be dangerous, but it is full of excitement and pleasure.'

He led the boy over harsh rocks and through wooded thickets. Eventually they arrived safely in the marketplace of the town. Darkness was falling and farmers from the surrounding area were making their way home, so there was nothing to buy. In spite of that the place was full of life. From restaurants came the smell of cooking food and many people were trying their luck at the gambling tables. A number of vendors were offering wine and spirits for sale. Next to the entrance of one magnificent house, white blossoms sent out their tantalizing scent.

The thief led the pupil to one of the playing tables, where they were welcomed on all sides.

'Here you are again! Where have you been all this time?' asked a bearded man.

'I've been in the temple,' came the answer.

'Then you certainly won't have any money for gambling today.'

'Oh yes I have,' said the boy confidently. He was about to throw the monks' money on to the table.

'You mustn't do that!' said the pupil.

'Let me do it,' the boy said, trying to calm him.

When the game was finished, he had won double his stake money and he showed off his winnings to his friend.

'But what would have happened if you had lost?' asked the worried pupil.

'But I haven't lost and now we can buy double what the monks asked for.'

'You can't buy anything more today. Everything's closed. So what shall we do now?'

'Follow me and I'll show you something that will be a completely new experience for you.'

Together they entered the House of the Scented Jasmine. The pupil had never seen so many beautiful young women and was enchanted. The young thief greeted each girl by name and introduced them to his friend. He said to them, 'Be particularly nice to my friend. This is his first time.' Then he said to the pupil, 'Pick the one you like and we'll enjoy ourselves.'

The boys made their choice and took the two girls into a room where a sumptuous dinner was laid out. The girls made sure that they catered for their companions' every wish. During the evening the young thief took his companion into another room.

'I wish you a good night!' he said to his friend, who remained sitting in the dining room and wondered what to do now. The girl wanted him to go with her but he wanted to leave this house as quickly as possible because he now felt that he was in great danger. During the night he wandered around town and many images flashed through his mind. He remembered how he and his Master had surprised the boy in the act of stealing the statues. He saw scenes from his youth and from the time in the temple and suddenly he saw the face of the beautiful girl with long black hair. He asked himself whether he should have followed his mate, though he didn't even want to think what he might be up to right now. At the same time he was annoyed to have missed such a great opportunity.

'There's still time to go back,' he thought, but then he pulled himself together and started to look for a sheltered place to sleep.

The next morning he was roughly shaken. As he opened his eyes he saw the thief standing in front of him looking agitated.

'Wake up,' he said. 'We must decide what we want to do now. The girl told me that you didn't stay last night. That was silly of you because I had already paid for both of us and I can't get a refund, so we have no money left.'

'What have you done?!' the terrified pupil shouted.

'What I've done you have also done, almost,' answered the boy.

'But we can't go back without completing our errand.'

'Why not?'

'Because the monks trusted us with that money and we haven't spent it as we were told.'

'We could say that we lost it, or that it got stolen.'

'But that would mean lying, as well. And we are harming the monks because we aren't bringing them any food.'

The pupil looked at his friend angrily. Finally the thief said, 'It's easy, we'll just steal what we need.'

'Now you want to steal, as well!' shouted the pupil in alarm.

'Have you a better idea?' asked the boy provokingly.

The pupil stayed silent.

'That'll do it. Let me sort it out,' said the boy.

It was time for evening prayer when the two returned to the temple. The Master saw that they had completed their task and said, 'It is difficult to live on the opposite side of people. But it is even harder to be amongst them. The most difficult is to deny yourself the pleasures that human society can provide.'

The two boys looked anxious but remained silent, because they did not know what effect the Master expected his words to have. Then he brought them a meal and said, 'You must be tired, now eat and have a rest.'

The path is in yourself.

DURING THE FOLLOWING days the boys were seized by an unfamiliar restlessness. They asked themselves whether the Master knew about their misadventure and, if not, whether they should confess.

One morning the Master called them and said, 'No one can live a life without faults. Someone who commits a fault is like a wanderer who has lost his way and reached a roaring river that he has to cross. Then he sees a bridge and is happy to have discovered it but, having reached the opposite shore, he still doesn't know what path to take in order to reach his destination.'

When the pupil and the thief heard these words, they feared they would be punished because they thought the Master's words applied to them. But he continued, 'If you want to know which is the right path, you should repaint the whole wall around the temple.'

In the following days the boys were seen only at morning and evening prayers. The rest of the time they worked at painting the wall, even though the task appeared endless. One time the Master passed and asked, 'Have you seen the river yet?'

The boys said they hadn't and the Master left without any comment.

In the following weeks the lads became one with the rhythm of their work. They were proud of what they had achieved so far but, looking at the task ahead, they doubted whether they had sufficient energy. When the Master came by again, he asked once more, 'Have you seen the river yet?'

'Yes,' said the boys. Then the Master asked, 'And have you found the bridge?' They shook their heads silently and, once more, the Master left without comment.

The longer the lads worked on the wall, the less notice they took of their surroundings. They only saw the paint that they applied. Their world had turned white.

When the Master returned, he asked, 'Have you found that bridge yet?'

'Yes,' replied the lads.

'And have you also found the way that you have to take?'

The boys said no and carried on painting the wall, until one day they couldn't even see the paint any more. Then the Master came back to them and asked, 'Have you found the path you have to take?' Both nodded silently. Then the Master said, 'If you know which way brought you here, then you also know which way to go and you can cross the bridge.'

'You mustn't confuse the way you came for the way you will go on,' said the pupil. 'The path is in yourself and you don't even need a bridge.'

The young thief added, 'I see clearly both where I have come from and where I am going, but I want to take time to cross the bridge.'

The Master struck the floor with his stick and called out, 'The task is complete! From now on you can return to your usual work.'

If one has both knowledge and wisdom, the lamp illuminates even the darkest night.

SINCE THE PUPIL had discovered the secret of inner immersion he didn't regard the work of carrying water as arduous any longer, but saw it as an opportunity to increase his mental and physical strength. Prayers morning and evening added strength to his soul and the daily meals meant more to him than merely acquiring nourishment. They helped him to understand the context of life. He always thought of the grain of rice he had eaten at the beginning of his journey. Each moment he devoted to the practice of silent contemplation, and he could not imagine ever wanting to live differently.

The other boy, the former thief, had changed so much since his return to the temple that he had earned the respect and affection of all, which was something he had lacked for so long. Everybody, even the abbot, was now convinced that no one is bad by nature and that water is never contaminated at its source.

One evening after prayers, the Master said to his pupil, 'One should never get used to a place where you live because, otherwise, it takes possession of you. Whoever is attached to something will have sorrows, and he who has sorrows is unable to embrace wisdom. We will leave this place tomorrow.'

The boy was disappointed. Not only because he had to give up his new home, but also because he had to leave his young friend behind.

'The worth of friendship is invisible,' said the Master as though he knew what his pupil was feeling.

'But there are so many books here that I have not yet studied,' the boy wailed. 'How can I just leave them behind unread?'

The Master smiled. 'And what if one had read them all?'

'Then one has found wisdom,' answered the pupil.

'Don't confuse wisdom with knowledge,' said the Master. 'You may find knowledge in books but wisdom only in the heart. Knowledge without wisdom is like a lamp you hold in your hand that cannot be lit. Wisdom without knowledge is like a flame that goes out quickly when deprived of oil. Only if one has both knowledge and wisdom will the lamp illuminate even the darkest night.'

The boy had no answer. He wished his Master goodnight and extinguished his lamp. He dreamed that all the monks of the temple were electing his friend, the former thief, as the new abbot.

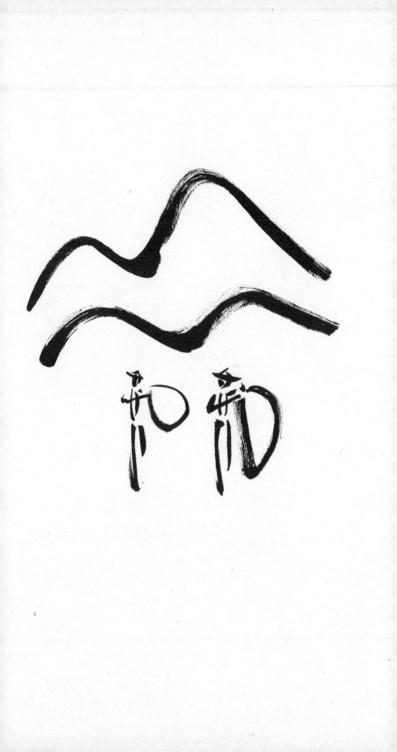

As long as you are without fear, danger avoids you.

BEFORE SUNRISE, THE Master and his pupil left the temple and climbed down the mountain. They reached a crossing and decided to take the way leading to a plain. After some time they reached a bridge over a gorge. The spars of the bridge had been severely rotted by wind and rain. The boy was afraid and, pausing, looked helplessly at his Master.

'How shall we cross?' he wanted to know.

'Who do you trust more, the bridge or yourself?' asked the Master.

'I don't know.'

'Would you dare to cross if the spars didn't look so rotten?'

'Of course.'

'But who tells you that you'd get across safely?'

The boy didn't answer.

'If you are afraid, you can trust neither the bridge nor yourself. Remember, as long as you are without fear, danger avoids you.'

After they had crossed the gorge their path led them to a marketplace. It was the only one in the area. Here the inhabitants of all the surrounding villages came together, some to sell their goods and others to buy, to exchange news and to meet friends and acquaintances. Street musicians entertained and jugglers amazed everyone with their tricks. There was a confusion of people, animals, colours, smells, and sounds. In all this confusion there was one person whose long hair had been gathered into a long plait. On the ground was a cloth, and on this had been placed apricots, peaches, plums, almonds and fresh vegetables for sale. When the boy saw the girl he couldn't prevent a recurrence of the strange feeling he'd had when he met her before. He left the Master and ran to the girl. Their meeting was like the recognition of two souls who remembered their original unity only vaguely.

'Are you already a Master?' the girl asked.

At this moment the Master arrived and said, 'You can only become a Master if you follow the path of the Light. It is not easy. You can find it in love, but that is not enough. You can find it in faith, but that is also not enough. By following the path one can find liberation.

'But love makes you happy,' the girl said.

'Happiness turns you into a slave because there will come a day when it leaves you. Then you will long for it, can't find it and will drown in sorrow. You can only be truly happy if you renounce happiness.'

Then the Master turned and walked away.

Darkness had nearly fallen when the boy caught up with the Master on his way to the Light.

The more often you fill your bowl, the hungrier you will be.

O N THEIR WAY they had seen dried-up farmland, scorched deserts, snow-covered peaks, dried-up river beds, flooded plains, and burned forests. They also passed mountain springs, reedy lakes, summer fields and meadows sparkling with dew.

The pupil had become used to eating only once a day at most, to spending the night in the shelter of trees or caves, to knowing no real home, and to keeping warm in spite of torn clothes. During his search for the Treasure of Life he thought sometimes trouble had already found him by meeting the girl, but then he remembered the words his Master had spoken long ago: 'Water in a spring longs to become one with the sea, but until this is fulfilled one must endure some physical and mental pain, and torture of the spirit.'

Towards noon the two wanderers reached a village in an area where everything seemed to grow in profusion. It was warm and the snow was long gone. In front of some of the huts, meals were just being prepared. The Master and his pupil came to a fireside, where they were invited to join the family for a meal. Since the boy had left his own village no one had offered him such delicacies. He sat beside the Master and stared at the food. Something stopped him from eating. The Master, who noticed his hesitation, said, 'I know that you are thinking of your home village and your family. You are sad because this meal and the people here remind you of your past. But as long as you carry it in your memory it remains alive and you have not really lost it. You have not left your home at all. The past is like a spark, which you can either extinguish or allow to become a mighty flame. And now eat!'

When the Master saw that the boy now gulped the food avidly, he warned him, 'The more often you fill your bowl, the hungrier you will be. Only when you can empty it with effort have you found the right measure. The earth gives us everything that we need. So why do we still want more?'

These words annoyed the host so much that he jumped up and shouted, 'We offer you the best we have and you don't appreciate it! You clearly envy us our wealth. We work hard for what we have but you just wander around and expect us to support your begging.'

The Master just smiled but, before he could reply, the pupil said, 'Please forgive us, we are not ungrateful. We thank you and we thank the earth which has presented us with such wealth. There are those who work hard to become rich, others work to become happy, and some work to become free. Everyone is aiming for a goal. But will they be contented when they have reached it? No, for then they strive for a new goal. The rich want to be richer, the happy try to be happier, and the free struggle to find greater freedom. But if you understand that the law of the earth consists of being there for others, then you know that we all need help, no matter whether we are rich or poor, old or young, beautiful or ugly, strong or weak. If we get no help we aren't able to live. We can only live properly if we help others.'

So the Master and the pupil prepared to travel on. As they said goodbye to the family, the father said, 'If your path brings you this way again, don't forget to visit us.'

After they had walked for a while in silence the Master said to the pupil, 'Soon there will be a time when you don't need me any more.'

I will be the sun of your smile and the tears of your grief.

IT HAD BEEN raining for days. Their shoes were sodden and the water dripped from their cloaks. When the rain eased off and the sun came out, it got so unbearably hot that they longed for the rain again. In this high place it was impossible to shelter from the forces of nature. They could do nothing but follow their path. The rocks were so slippery that they had to tread carefully in order to avoid slipping and falling to the depths below.

When the rain ceased the Master came to a halt. He looked at the boy and said, 'My child, from now on you will continue alone. But even if you don't see me any more I will still be with you. I will watch over you when you lie sleeplessly at night and I will enter your dreams when you finally fall asleep. I will help you when you are in danger and I will share your happiness when you give help to others. I will be with you when you are unsure of your way, even though your goal lies nearby. I will be the sun of your smile and the tears of your grief, which you will transform into strength. This will assist you to find the Treasure of Life. And when you have found it, it will help you to pass it on. Remember this: there is nothing that comes and nothing that goes. Everything is always there, the beginning and the end are one. The Great Circle turns by itself. Nothing started it and it will never be still. Everything is in the Great Circle and everything will be in the Great Circle. Movement is life and movement is death. Life is sorrow, death is sorrow. Sorrow is grief and pain. Grief and pain hide wisdom. Wisdom is liberation from passion. Liberation from passion is the finding of moderation. Moderation is Right Joy. The Right Joy is Right Giving. The Right Giving is Right Understanding. The Right Understanding awakens in the arms of time.'

The rain began again and became so heavy that the boy could scarcely see the Master. In spite of that, he clearly heard his voice saying, 'Don't be sad. The sun, which sinks below the horizon, will be reborn at the horizon. And the lake, which lies in the midst of the mountains, will announce its coming.'

The pupil saw the figure of the Master turn and disappear into the pouring rain. At this moment a huge chunk of rock came loose from the mountain peak and crashed to the valley. Further rocks broke off and crashed to the depths smashing everything in their path. The whole mountain started to move, accompanied by a rumble that united with the thunderous sound of the falling rocks and reached a terrible crescendo. Darkness was everywhere and destruction triumphed over life.

The shepherds in the valley who had heard and felt the unleashed forces of nature from afar herded the sheep

into their pens, then rushed to the site of the disaster
with their dogs as quickly as they could. They climbed
over fallen rocks and splintered tree trunks to look for
those who were buried. One of the dogs dug until it found
the boy. Working with all their might, they cleared the
rock and stones away and dragged him from the rubble.

'I know him,' a shepherd shouted, 'but he was certainly
not alone. He has been travelling the land with his
Master for many years. Once I even shared my meal with
them. Come quickly: we must find the old man as well!'

Carefully they carried the boy to a meadow and laid him
down. The one who had recognized him stayed with him
while the others ran back to look for the Master. Later
they carried the boy to a stable and laid him on a bed of
straw. When they were sure that he was uninjured, they
covered him with blankets and let him sleep.

After sleeping for three days and three nights, he awoke
and asked the man who was with him, 'Where are your
sheep?'

'They are asleep.'

'Where is my Master?'

The man was silent. After a while he said, 'I think he is also asleep.'

'Do you know where he sleeps?' asked the boy.

'I don't know. We have searched for him for days but we only found this stick.'

The following days and nights the boy spent in prayer. He refused to eat, drink or sleep. Constantly he thought of his Master and repeated all the prayers and chants he had learned in the temple. Finally he fell once more into a deep sleep and after that his body recovered.

The shepherd was seated on his horse on top of a mound and watched the young man as he strode off through the valley. All he carried was a stick of sandalwood.

Who will lead him now?

IN THE EARLY evening he reached the village square. He passed the fountain and climbed the stone steps of the temple. Then he entered the prayer hall and knelt in prayer. After collecting his thoughts for a moment, he suddenly felt as though there was someone behind him. For a moment he hoped that it was his Master. He didn't dare to turn round because he feared disappointment.

'I've been told that a young man carrying a stick was praying here,' he heard a voice whisper behind him. 'And now I have come to see whether this is my son, who left his father's house long ago to pursue the way of wisdom with his Master.'

He turned round and looked into the eyes of his mother.

While they walked home together she told him, 'Your brother married the cobbler's daughter, and they have two little girls. Although your father would have preferred a grandson he is not disappointed, because he thinks that granddaughters will not go so far away from home later.'

These made the boy doubt for the first time whether he had fulfilled his obligations as a son.

'All the servants are still with us,' continued his mother,

'and we have more animals than ever. The men can hardly get all the work done.'

Even before they entered the house they were seen by the two girls, who shouted excitedly, 'Grandmother has a strange man with her.' At once his brother went to greet them and for a moment the two stood looking at each other in silence. Then they embraced, and with his brother the boy entered his parents' house after many years once again.

Later, as they sat around the dinner table, everyone wanted to give the boy special food and take the chance to greet him properly. The cobbler's daughter said, 'I hope that from now on you'll stay with us. Look at your brother: since he's been married and has children he's fully content. Children are the treasure of life. You should also find a wife and settle down. Look, you're so thin and your shoes are in a terrible state! I will make you some new ones.'

A servant brought in delicacies. The smell reminded the boy of former times. He saw himself sitting at the table as a child and saw that the seats of his grandparents had now been taken by his parents.

'I'm happy that today my family is reunited,' said the

mother. 'And I'm happy that whilst one of our sons ensured that the family will continue, the other has been searching for Wisdom. His father has read many books but could not find the wisdom in them. Now we hope that our son will succeed. That's why we won't be sad when he leaves us again tomorrow to follow his path.'

Then the father spoke. 'We respect your decision to lead a life that is not in the tradition of our family. I am happy that I can see you one more time and I know that you won't bring shame upon us.'

'He tells me that he hasn't got a Master any more,' said the brother, 'so should he really leave us again? And who will lead him now?'

The next morning came unwillingly.

THE NEWS OF the boy's return reached all the houses in the village. Many of the villagers stood outside his parents' house hoping to catch a glimpse of him. When one of his former friends saw this he decided to avoid them by entering the house through the back door. He arrived in the middle of a family gathering, and after saying hello he announced, 'I brought dessert! Freshly baked in my own shop. Tomorrow you really must visit me. My shop is the best in the village, and my son is the best in the whole school. Nobody calls him "Strawhead"!'

The family invited him to stay. Now he told his friend everything that had happened since he left and what had become of their mutual friends. He also told of the mule driver who had left the village and made his fortune. It was rumoured, however, that his riches were not the proceeds of honest work. The two of them talked for ages, and when the visitor at last said goodbye he asked, 'Is one really without sorrow after giving up everything?'

By now it was late. The crowd in front of the house went home without having seen the boy. The two girls and their parents went to bed. But three people stayed awake in the house the whole night.

The next morning came unwillingly. The family gathered quietly in front of the house. Even the dogs did not bark.

He now knew where his path would be leading him.

WITH MANY NEW canvas shoes in his luggage, the young man moved on. He wanted to continue on the Master's path and bring the people the Treasure of Life. But where should he find it? Was he even able to do so, now that he was alone?

More and more his doubts tormented him. Should he stay in the mountains or would it be better to journey into the valley? Should he join other wanderers or once again enter a temple? Was it really right that he had left his family and friends? Couldn't he make himself more useful in the village than on the country road?

The more he thought about his future, the weaker he became. By the time evening came, he felt so ill that he collapsed at the edge of the path. He no longer even had the strength to look for a place to sleep. Heat and cold tormented his body and he shivered like a young tree tossed mercilessly in a heavy storm. Finally he fell into a deep sleep ...

He saw a beautiful girl coming towards him from afar. She waved to him and he ran towards her. When he was quite near her, she suddenly disappeared. But shortly afterwards he saw her running to the river and again she waved to him. He ran after her as fast as he could, but was not able to catch up with her. When she arrived at the banks she brazenly stripped naked and jumped into the floods. The young man also jumped into the river and swam after her. He had nearly caught up with her and wanted to grab her by her plait when she dived under and swam away. And again he followed her. Now the river became much deeper and faster. Suddenly he lost sight of the girl and a powerful current took hold of his body. Desperately he tried to free himself and managed to hold on to a branch, on which he could pull himself to the banks ...

The young man woke up. His hand held the Master's stick so tightly it seemed as though he would never let go again.

Morning had broken. He felt full of vigour and strode on without wavering. He now knew where his path would be leading him.

My knife knows no patience.

I N THE YEARS following his training the young man became so famous that his reputation raced ahead of him. Wherever he went, people eagerly invited him to stay because they were keen to share his knowledge. But he stayed nowhere long.

One day he came to a village that looked very run-down. Only a single house, which appeared to belong to someone wealthy, was in good repair. The young man was curious and, just as he was passing, a servant ran out and, in the name of his Master, begged him to enter. He followed the servant and was led into a hall.

'I knew it must be you,' came a voice from behind. 'I've heard a lot about you since you left the village.'

The young man turned round and was confronted with the mule driver from his childhood village. The man had aged and now had only one leg.

'One leg's gone,' he said, 'but look at what else I have: a huge house, servants, many concubines, golden plates, a silk gown and a stable full of horses.'

The man ordered his servants to prepare lunch. Then he led his guest into a hidden room that was filled with cases and weapons.

'I'm offering you the chance of a lifetime. Since I lost my leg I need a partner to help with my business. I've heard of your success and it's clear to me that you could be the right person. First, you're young enough, second, you're strong enough, and third, you're some sort of holy man.'

The young man wanted to interrupt but the mule driver didn't give him the chance.

'As you can see, I've found a way to get rich quickly. But first, I want to tell you how I lost my leg. For years I have been smuggling forbidden goods across the border. A few months ago, on a stormy night, I was following a steep track with my fully laden mules when, suddenly, one of the animals behind me slipped and fell down the slope. I was holding the reins and could not let go in time so I was dragged down with the animal. We hit the ground at the same time but the mule fell on my leg. The animal was dead, but I survived the fall, even though it was two days before anyone found me and got me to a doctor. Sadly, he couldn't save my leg.'

The man patted his remaining leg and said, 'It's not so bad for me to live with one leg when I think what I have got from my work so far: money, lots of it. And now my loss doesn't seem so bad because I know that my son will inherit more than poverty.'

'Why don't you make your son your successor?' the young man asked.

'My son has become a border guard and it is already hard enough for him to avoid denouncing me. And don't think that I can trust my servants! Why do you think we're staying in this hidden room? And don't go thinking that my wives really love me. All they want is for me to die and leave them my money. You are the only one I can trust. That's why I'm begging you to take up my offer. Then I'll no longer be alone.'

The smuggler waited for a reaction but none was forthcoming. He tried again. 'Think of what you'll gain! I'm offering you more than half and you'll be able to buy whatever you want.'

When the young man still said nothing, his companion suddenly pulled a knife and threatened him. Then he shouted angrily, 'Now you already know too much, so either you agree or I'll have to kill you!'

Still the young man did not react and this put the smuggler in an even greater rage.

'You'd better say something, because my knife knows no patience!'

The young man got up, gazed at the smuggler for a while and then said, 'Each action has its time. Each time is of a certain length. If you run quicker than both, nobody will be able to help you.'

The mule driver recognized with whom he had talked and he asked respectfully, 'Will you not let me call you "Master"?'

At that moment there was a knocking at the door. A servant called, 'The meal is ready,' and he heard the guest say, 'Thank you.'

'In mourning.'

AGAIN AUTUMN HAD come. The young man arrived at a village where there had just been a great harvest. He passed through orchards and suddenly he remembered how he and his Master had been welcomed in this place a long time ago. Then it had been spring, but now everything was getting ready for nature's long sleep.

As he walked he noticed a poor-looking house where people were coming and going. Drawing near he saw that people were fixing a white sign to the door on which was written in black ink, 'In mourning'. Suddenly he recognized the house again. He made his way through the orchard and entered. Inside, he found the girl kneeling by the bier of her blind grandfather.

The people in the house cried without cease. The young man went up to them and said, 'Be without sorrow and dry your tears. He isn't dead. He is merely resting in the arms of nature before coming back renewed. He who leaves his body needs seven times seven days to find his new destination. But he will only succeed if his relatives, friends and dependants help him through their prayers.'

He became silent. Then he quietly spoke some words to encourage the old man's return. The girl fetched candles and incense sticks and lit them. Again she knelt in front of the grandfather and looked expectantly at the young man.

'Are we both completely alone now?' she asked.

'Each of us is alone,' he answered. 'At the times we are not alone, we fail to recognize the value of togetherness. Children do not recognize the value of their parents, their siblings or their relatives. Men do not recognize the value of their wives, and friends do not see the worth of their friends. The healthy do not appreciate their health and the living do not know the value of life. The dead show us just how precious all living things are. That is why death is an immeasurably great treasure.'

The girl lifted her head, looked hopefully at the young man and grasped his hand.

A few days later they chose a small knoll not far from the house as the site of the grandfather's grave. At the foot of the knoll they planted a ginkgo tree. From afar it looked as though its branches touched the sky.

'I cannot leave you alone,' said the young man one evening as the girl stuck new candles into the candlesticks and renewed the incense sticks. 'I want to stay with you and look after you.'

The girl sadly shook her head and said, 'That is not possible, because you must not abandon the path you have been treading even if you are full of passion. My grandfather once said, "Passion is like wine: the more you drink the drunker you get. But when you wake up from your drunkenness the dream has gone. Friendship, on the other hand, is like water. At first you think you cannot relish it, but in time you learn to appreciate its good taste."' The girl stopped for a moment and then continued, 'We can't stay together because I don't want to give you either my passion or my friendship but my love, and love means to make life better for the loved one and not chain him to yourself. That is why you have to move on. Only then you will find what you seek.'

After forty-nine days, when the ashes of the grandfather were buried under the ginkgo tree and his soul had found its final destination, the girl brought the young man the Master's stick and said, 'It's time to leave.' She gave him a ginkgo leaf. Then she led him out to the main road and said, 'Go now! Go on your way! Even when we are parted we will grow together. And we will find each other when the dew of the new day moistens our souls. And we will return in a new form to become one in the Great Circle.'

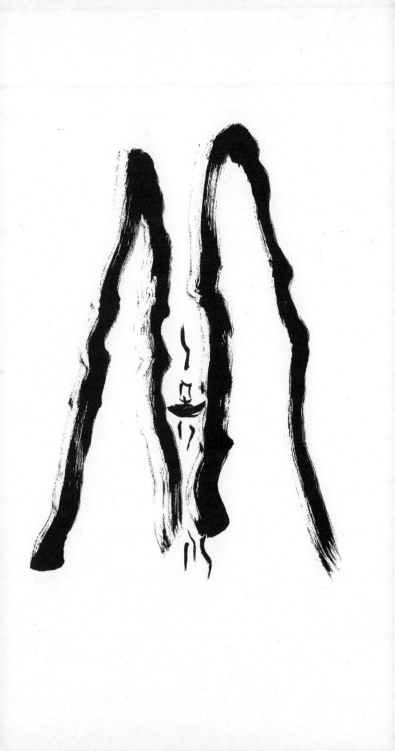

The great storm should lead him south.

THE GREAT STORM should lead him south. His soul obeyed the orders of the winds and the keel of the boat drew a straight line in the calm waters. He entered houses supported on piles, in front of which women washed their laundry in the river, while their children played on the banks and splashed in the shallows. He passed fields where farmers were planting rice, and floating markets where people sold fruit and vegetables, fish, meat and spices. From some you could even buy clothes, household goods and toys. Then the boat scudded past fishing nets before finally reaching the dreaded rapids.

The landscape changed suddenly. The river had become narrow. Pointed rocks jutted out of the water and there were dangerous whirlpools where those who managed to pass unscathed regarded themselves as lucky. In place of the shallow banks there were now steep rocky walls that climbed so high that the sky could only be glimpsed through a tiny cleft. Suddenly a mighty whirlpool grabbed hold of the boat and started to fling it back and forth like a leaf. The more he wrestled with the rudder the more it resisted him, and the boat was keeling over dangerously so that the mast nearly struck the rocks.

A moment later the danger was over. The river became calm, allowing a respite. Soon he could moor the boat.

He has started this journey because an invitation from the Emperor had reached him. He was invited to come to see him in the town of a Thousand Lotus Lakes because the Emperor needed his advice. He was reluctant to go at first, because his Master had always warned him against the rich and mighty. Eventually, however, his need to share his knowledge with others overruled his existing qualms.

He was thinking this over when he was surprised by a loud hissing, and suddenly saw a huge paw with great sharp claws right in front of him. He quickly assumed a defence position that he had practised countless times when he was at the temple. His opponent was a mighty mountain lion which, baring his teeth, was preparing to spring and attack. But suddenly he paused as a mysterious power hindered his plan. He stared at the man, who stood before him completely motionless. The mountain lion felt itself unable to move.

'I could kill you now with my mind,' said the young man, 'but I won't. For every creature there is a right time and place to die. You must leave this place, however, and to show you that I am serious I will give you a warning.'

With that a heavy bough from a tree up above them suddenly came crashing down right beside the mountain lion where he stood. The young man picked up the Master's stick and, pointing firmly with it, commanded the frightened mountain lion to leave immediately in that direction.

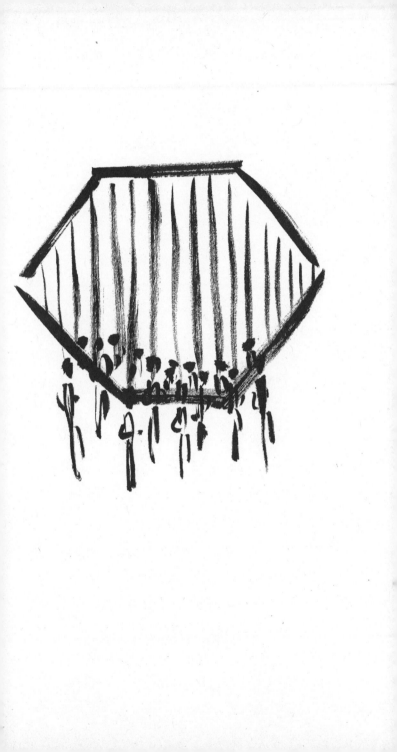

I am ready, Master!

O N THE ROAD leading into the Town of the Thousand Lotus Lakes, men carrying a sedan approached him and asked him, in the name of the Emperor, to climb in.

When they reached the palace, the whole royal household was assembled to welcome the guest. From the towers of the palace walls fanfares sounded to announce his arrival. Flags were raised and the soldiers formed a parade. A footman pulled the curtains of the sedan apart and helped him to climb out. Then an official appeared, wearing a golden seal of office, and led him through richly ornamented courtyards to a place to which few ever gained admission.

'Do you know how it feels to be an Emperor?' he heard a youthful voice ask.

'Why do you want to know?' he replied.

'I have called for you to learn how best to rule my country.'

'And what makes you think I would know?'

'I have heard extraordinary things about you!'

'But is that any reason why I should be the right man to teach you?'

'Nobody else has the knowledge you possess.'

'It takes more than knowledge to rule a country."

'But nobody has seen so much of life as you on your wanderings.'

'I am still on my way.'

'Then will you not rest here awhile?'

'I do not want to interrupt my journey.'

'Not even if I need your help? And if with that help I could turn my country into the best of all countries and my people into the happiest of all people?'

'As long as you think these people are "your" people, they cannot become happy, and as long as they are not happy they will not be able to serve their country with all their power.'

'But it is necessary to keep order!'

'Order should not be kept merely by law, but by insight.'

'And how do you find this insight?'

'You must get to know life.'

'Teach me how to live!' the Emperor pleaded.

'Climb down from your throne,' the Master ordered, 'and leave the palace. Take off your magnificent robes and live with the poor. Put your jade chopsticks aside and eat with the peasants. Leave your four-poster bed and sleep on nature's floor. Avoid your sedans and move your legs. Keep away from the concubines and live like a monk. See the light and the dark. Get to know the warmth and the cold. Examine the soft and the hard. Taste the sweet and the bitter. Feel the beautiful and the ugly.'

The Master stopped, glared at the Emperor piercingly and said, 'Touch the old, touch the sick, touch the dead and touch the newborn!'

The Emperor got up and climbed slowly down the steps of his throne. He took off his crown and let his dragon robe drop. Then he said: 'I am ready, Master!

In that case, said the Master, 'I will take a rest here.'

Then he saw a single grain of rice begin to ripen.

THE MASTER SPENT the whole summer in the Town of a Thousand Lotus Lakes before moving on. On his way he saw how rulers lost their power and how their successors argued over who should be the next ruler.

He saw how fathers and sons fought and killed each other.

He saw how the best advisors were executed by their employers.

He saw how the unscrupulous grabbed the highest offices in the state.

He saw how the bravest soldiers, who had persevered the longest, were cut down by their enemies and had their heads hung in the wind as a deterrent.

He saw how the hands and feet of those who had fought for the truth were tortured with nails.

He saw how the wisest men were forced to drink poisoned wine.

He saw how the truth was turned into lies.

He saw how they traded something round for something that was square.

He saw the best doctors arrested and their knowledge wiped out.

He saw how the most important manuscripts were burned.

He saw how the common folk slaughtered each other without reason.

He saw how even the most holy women were taken by force.

He saw how women were forced to sell their bodies.

He saw soldiers slit open the stomachs of pregnant women with their bayonets.

He saw how people gambled all their possessions in return for fleeting pleasure.

He saw families driven apart and stripped of their possessions.

He saw how whole populations were forced to obey their conquerors.

He saw how huge areas of the best land were laid waste so that the people starved.

He saw the holy places burned and the sanctuaries turned to ashes.

He saw teachers forced to spread lies.

He saw the greatest thieves honoured as heroes.

He saw how the best students, who had fought for people's rights, were slaughtered by engines of death.

He saw a mass murderer become an idol to a whole generation.

He saw great inventions that pulled their creators into the abyss.

He saw burning earth.

He saw burning water.

He saw burning air.

He saw life in flames.

He moved on.

He crossed a burned field. The wind blew ashes across the ruined land. And then he saw a single grain of rice begin to ripen.

Even when we are parted we will grow together.

MANY YEARS LATER the Master reached the river of memories. Lying on the ground he stared at the sky and followed the movement of the clouds with his eyes. The rays of the sun warmed him and he eventually fell into a deep sleep.

When he woke up he wandered to the place where, in his younger years, he thought he had found happiness. From afar he saw the crown of the ginkgo tree. He climbed the hill and viewed the landscape. In the plain, next to old farms, he saw many newly built houses, which all looked alike and were connected by roads beside which electricity pylons ran in a row.

Opposite the hill lay the cemetery of the village. On one of the gravestones he saw the name of the grandfather, and on another, next to the ginkgo tree, he found the name of the girl. His sight became dim and it seemed that he heard a familiar voice whispering, 'Whatever will happen, we can't avoid it. And whatever won't happen, we can't force it. Everything happens because it has to happen.'

He didn't know how long he stood there motionless, when suddenly a child's voice brought him back to the present. A little boy wanted to lay a bunch of white chrysanthemums on the grave.

'Who are you,' the child asked, 'and what are you doing here?'

'Who are you, and what are you doing here?' the Master retorted.

'I'm giving flowers to my grandmother,' the boy answered.

'And where is your grandfather?' the Master asked.

'I don't know.'

'But you know where your father is?'

'Of course. At home with my mother. Do you want to meet my parents?'

The farm had undergone many changes over the years. It now looked as if it had only just been built. At the entrance a man greeted him warmly and said, 'I have been waiting for this moment for a long time.' Then he carried on sadly, 'My mother thought of you until her last breath. But she had promised me that you would return one day and she also said that you would bring something special with you.'

The little boy saw how the eyes of the old man brightened, and he heard him say, 'You're right. This is why I have come. It is also the reason why I am going away very soon. '

The family was disappointed that the guest, who had only just arrived, was already talking of leaving, but they all asked, 'Will you come back?'

Instead of an answer the Master gave the boy a box wrapped in cloth.

When he had disappeared in the distance, they took off the cloth and opened the box. It contained a book in which there lay a dried ginkgo leaf and in which was written with a fine brush:

'Even when we are parted
we will grow together.
And we will find each other
when the dew of the new day
moistens our souls.
And we will return in a new form
to become one in the Great Circle.'

FOG, IMPENETRABLE FOG. Day after day. No sound is heard. His feelings have become as still as the breath of nature. He steps slowly. In the mist a figure comes towards him. When they nearly touch, he hears the words: 'Look at the sky!' At this moment a powerful wind comes up and pulls the fog apart. He turns round but no one is to be seen. The fog has completely disappeared.

Sky, blue sky.

Blue sky without clouds.

FINALLY: THE SUN.